Triangular signs with a red bor̶d̶⟶ ͏le circular signs bordere͏⟶ will also see blue circular ͏⟶ 'll find them all in the Hig̶⟶

20 MPH SPEED L̶

(20)

Points: 5

̶ ̶ ̶ SPEED LIMIT

(30)

Points: 5

40 MPH SPEED LIMIT

(40)

Points: 5

50 MPH SPEED LIMIT

(50)

Points: 5

60 MPH SPEED LIMIT

(60)

Points: 5

NATIONAL SPEED LIMIT

Points: 5

Watch out for these triangular warning signs.

CATTLE

Points: 15

HORSES

Points: 15

SHEEP

Points: 15

HELICOPTER

Points: 15

ROADWORKS

Points: 15

SIDE WINDS

Points: 15

HUMP BRIDGE

Points: 15

TUNNEL

Points: 15

RIVERSIDE BRIDGE

Points: 15

PEDESTRIAN CROSSING

Points: 15

SLIPPERY SURFACE

Points: 15

TRAFFIC LIGHT

Points: 15

FALLING ROCKS

10 Points: 10

NO MOTORISED VEHICLES

10 Points: 10

NO OVERTAKING

10 Points: 10

NO CYCLING

10 Points: 10

NO PEDESTRIANS

10 Points: 10

NO U-TURN

10 Points: 10

These rectangular signs provide information regarding the area or road that you are about to enter.

Points: 10

RED ROUTE

Usually found in busy city and town centres, these are streets singled out for extra parking restrictions to keep the road free-flowing.

CONGESTION ZONE

Points: 15

LOW EMISSION ZONE

Points: 20

7

Here are some more information signs that are rectangular but with an arrow at one end. Look out for these brown tourist information signs.

MUSEUM

Points: 15

PICNIC AREA

Points: 10

ZOO

Points: 25

DRY-SKI SLOPE

Points: 35
Top Spot!

BEACH

Points: 15

COUNTRY PARK

Points: 10

ENGLISH HERITAGE

 Points: 20

VIEWPOINT

Points: 10

CASTLE

Points: 15

CRICKET GROUND

Points: 35
Top Spot!

CAMPSITE

Points: 10

TOURIST INFORMATION

Points: 5

BLUE MOTORWAY SIGN

Points: 5

All motorway signs are made in this special blue colour.

Points: 5

GREEN PRIMARY ROUTE SIGN

These are for main or A roads all around the country...

WHITE LOCAL ROUTE SIGN

Points: 5

...and these for local roads.

Points: 35 Top Spot!

PRE-WORBOYS SIGN

Nearly all UK road signs were modernised in 1964 by the Worboys Committee. A few escaped and are still present today.

OLD-FASHIONED

Points: 15

You are most likely to find these old fashioned signs in villages.

Points: 20

MAGIC ROUNDABOUT

A few of these complicated junctions exist in the UK. A cluster of small roundabouts surround a major one. They can be very confusing! This is a famous one in Swindon.

A gradient sign indicates the angle or steepness of a hill or incline. The higher the number, the steeper the hill. Some older road signs indicate the number as a fraction – 1:4 is the same as 25%. This actually means for every four units travelled horizontally, one unit is travelled up or down.

25% GRADIENT

Points: 20

In this case the sign advises the driver that a downhill section of road is approaching.

30% GRADIENT

In this case uphill with many other advisory instructions.

Points: 25

40% GRADIENT

A very steep downhill road.

Points: 30

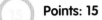

Points: 15

TRUCK ROUTE

A sign like this indicates the best route for trucks to take avoiding smaller side roads and helps prevent congestion.

BUS LANE

Points: 10

Bus lanes ensure that buses can travel freely during the busy rush hours. Often the main sign will be accompanied by another outlining which hours the bus lane operates.

Points: 15

TO THE SEAPORT

This way If you are catching a ferry.

RING ROAD

Points: 10

Many cities and towns have roads around them. This means that heavy traffic can avoid the city centre.

Points: 15

DIAMOND DIVERSION

There may be emergency roadworks on a main road. This diamond sign shows a diversion route.

FOOTPATH

Points: 10

Footpath signs are common in the country and can be seen along the roadside.

Points: 20
double if the town is twinned
with more than one place

TWINNED

Twinned towns or cities have close links or are usually twinned with similar places in other countries. Some places are twinned with towns from more than one country. Twinning can be used to promote tourism between the twinned towns.

Over the years there have been some fun examples of twinning including the village of Dull in Perthshire with Boring in Oregon, USA, and Wincanton in Somerset twinned with Ankh-Morpork from Terry Pratchett's Discworld.

15

BUS STOP

Points: 5

You are bound to find a bus stop in a street near you. Some, like this one, show several bus routes.

Points: 25

OUT OF ORDER BUS STOP

...but sometimes the bus stop may have to be taken out of service. This can happen if roadworks are being carried out.

PARK AND RIDE

Points: 10

Many towns and cities encourage motorists to park on the outskirts of town and travel to the centre by bus. 'Park and ride' schemes reduce the amount of city centre traffic, so buses and essential vehicles can move more freely.

Points: 10

PARENT AND CHILD PARKING

Most supermarkets have parent and child spaces, located close to the entrance.

PAY AND DISPLAY

Points: 10

Be sure to pay for parking where you see this sign.

Points: 10

VALUABLES

It is a good idea not to leave valuable items in the car.

MUSEUM

Points: 10
double if you go in one

Museums and galleries can be very popular – you may face a long queue to get in. Be patient – it will be worth it!

Points: 10
double if you go in one

THEATRE

A trip to the theatre is an exciting adventure.

Points: 10

Many shops have street-side displays showing their wares to foot and car passengers alike. Florists often have particularly pleasant displays.

Points: 10

There are different kinds of carwashes. The one shown here is a self-service automatic carwash which you drive through. With others, people will wash your car by hand using water jets. At some carwashes you are given the water jets but you must wash the car yourself!

MULTIPLEX CINEMA

Points: 10

Some multiplex cinemas can screen many films at the same time.

 Points: 10

LIBRARY

A great place to borrow a book, CD or DVD.

HOTEL

Points: 10

Many hotels are grand buildings, sometimes with hundreds of bedrooms, and form part of the local history.

Points: 20
double if you can identify
the monarch

Many towns and villages have statues of kings and queens.

MEMORIAL

Points: 15

Memorials are usually erected to remember those who have died in war or in conflict.

 Points: 25

EQUESTRIAN STATUE

Equestrian means 'on horseback' so look for a statue of a rider on a horse.

TOWN HALL

Points: 10

Town halls are normally grand buildings situated in the centre of town, often in a prominent position or overlooking an important square.

POSTING BOX

Points: 30

It's quite rare to see one of these old-fashioned posting boxes now – you may only find them outside a large town or city post office.

Points: 35 **Top Spot!**

WALL CLOCK

Many town centres throughout the country still have ornate public clocks, often near town halls or other public buildings.

23

MORRIS DANCING

Points: 25 25

A traditional style dating back hundreds of years, popular at village fêtes.

15 **Points: 15**

PUNCH AND JUDY

Good old-fashioned fun! You are most likely to see a Punch and Judy show at the seaside. This tradition dates back over 100 years.

BALLOON SELLER

Points: 20 20

Sometimes there are so many balloons that it is difficult to see the balloon seller!

Points: 15

TRACTOR

In the countryside you will often see a tractor either at work in a field or occasionally holding up the traffic as it travels back and forth to the farm.

COMBINE HARVESTER

Points: 20

Giant combine harvesters gather in wheat from the crops and bale the straw automatically.

Points: 15

BALES

After the grain has been harvested, the straw is left in round or oblong bales in the field.

25

FARM SHOP

Points: 15

Farm shops are usually attached to a farm where locally produced meat, vegetables and fruit are sold.

Points: 15

HORSEBOX

Horseboxes are needed to transport horses around the country and come in many shapes and sizes.

ROE DEER

One of our native deer, naturally shy they sometimes run across country roads at night.

 Points: 25

PONY

You can still find wild ponies in several areas of Britain.

 Points: 20

BADGER

Top Spot! **Points: 50**

Sadly you are most likely to see a dead badger killed on the road but occasionally they can be spotted alive, by the roadside.

FOX

Foxes are surprisingly common and often find their way into towns and gardens looking for food, especially at night.

 Points: 20

PHEASANT

Most often spotted strutting around verges and field boundaries. The males are more colourful than the females.

 Points: 10

RED KITE

Brought back from the brink of extinction, red kites can be seen in small flocks in some areas.

 Points: 25

BLACK-HEADED GULL

Flocks of gulls are often seen following the farmer's plough or at landfill sites looking for food.

 Points: 15

DOG VAN

These vehicles have a rooftop air vent to allow the dogs to breathe.

Points: 25

SKIP TRUCK

A great way to dispose of large quantities of waste.

Points: 15

RECOVERY TRUCK

Essential to keep the roads clear.

Points: 15

CONCRETE MIXER

The drum holding the wet concrete rotates during driving to makes sure it doesn't set before being delivered.

Points: 20

CONVERTIBLE

Points: 10

A fun way to travel when the sun is shining!

Points: 35   **Top Spot!**

KIT CAR

Kit cars are easily spotted as they look different to most other cars on the road and are some times referred to as replica cars.

CITY BIKES

Points: 10

These bikes-for-hire have been introduced to several UK cities and have been a great success. Pick one up at the train station and deposit it at your destination!

Points: 10

LORRY

Lorries are a common sight on UK roads picking up and delivering a wide range of goods like food products, manufactured items, livestock and raw materials. Many lorries started their journey in other countries and can be spotted by their unusual number plates.

CITROËN 2CV

The 'tin snail' was originally designed to carry French country folk and their cargoes of eggs across rutted fields!

Points: 25

MGB GT

You may see either an open-top roadster (convertible) or this GT coupe featuring a tailgate rear door.

Points: 20

LANDROVER (SERIES 1)

Many of these very popular off-road vehicles were originally designed for military purposes.

Points: 20

VW CAMPER VAN

Points: 25

You will often find lovingly restored VW vans at surfing beaches or at family picnic spots and viewpoints.

Points: 35 Top Spot!

FORD ANGLIA

This popular car has found a whole new lease of life since appearing in the *Harry Potter* books.

Martin Charles Hatch / shutterstock.com

ROAD SWEEPER

Points: 15 15

Arena Photo UK / Shutterstock.com

Man-made rubbish like plastic bags and natural debris such as leaves in the autumn gather at the roadside. Vehicles such as this road sweeper use special brushes and vacuums to keep the streets as clean as possible.

HORSE AND CART

Points: 30 30

Horses and Carts may used by sightseeing tourists, or sometimes for weddings.

34

Points: 35 Top Spot!

WEDDING CAR

Christian Mueller / Shutterstock.com

Wedding cars are easily recognisable due to the ribbons that adorn the bonnet. They are usually either very plush luxury cars or classic cars. Often the type of car chosen will have significance to the couple getting married.

Points: 15
double if it is pink

LIMOUSINE

Hired for special
occasions.

CARAVAN

Points: 10
for each

Caravans and camper
vans let you pack up and
take your home wherever
you like!

Points: 15

CAR WITH TRAILER

Trailers are a great way
to transport boats and
canoes.

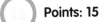
Points: 15

BOWLS

Bowls are weighted on one side so that they follow a curved line when rolled toward the jack.

CRICKET GROUND

Points: 10

You may see a game being played at a professional stadium or a more sedate game on a village green.

Points: 10

GOLF COURSE

Golf courses are found all over the country but particularly in the more rural parts of Scotland where the game was invented. Those by the sea are called links courses.

ATHLETICS TRACK

Points: 20

You may see a major competition at an athletics track.

 Points: 10

TENNIS COURT

Tennis courts can be found in many parks and in some private gardens!

OUTDOOR GYM

Points: 15

These are a great way to keep fit and have fun!

Points: 15

HORSE RACING TRACK

Horse racing attracts millions of visitors each year. Some courses have special races that are held annually and are shown on TV.

ICE RINK

Points: 20

Your local ice rink may host ice hockey matches or you may simply prefer to skate around to the music.

Points: 35 Top Spot!

Christophe Jossik / Shutterstock.com

DRY-SKI SLOPE

An ideal way to prepare for skiing on real snow.

39

Points: 5

L-PLATE

The traditional red on white L-plate denotes a learner driver.

P-PLATE

Points: 10

This P-plate shows that the vehicle is being driven by someone who has recently passed their driving test – a probationary driver.

DISABLED BADGE SIGN

Points: 5

Many places such as supermarkets save parking spots near the doors for people who have difficulty getting around – drivers who have a blue badge like this one displayed on their dashboard are allowed to park in these spaces.

Points: 15

BABY ON BOARD

Often people have a 'baby on board' sign on the back windscreen of their car. These help emergency services know to look for a small child in the event of an accident. Many people have more stylised signs saying things like 'little princess on board'. Score for any wording.

Cars from foreign countries can be identified by their number plates and an international registration badge. See how many of the following you can spy.

BELGIUM

B

Points: 15

FRANCE

F

Points: 10

GERMANY

D

Points: 10

HUNGARY

H

Points: 15

IRELAND

IRL

Points: 5

ITALY

I

Points: 15

JERSEY

Points: 25

NETHERLANDS

Points: 10

NORWAY

Points: 15

POLAND

Points: 15

SPAIN

Points: 15

SWITZERLAND

Points: 25

Since 1963 car registration numbers have denoted the year that the car was registered. Before this, they generally had three numbers and three letters. The letters were the designation of the area or city where the car had first been registered. In 1963 registrations had a letter added to denote the year: ABC 123 A, then in 1964, ABC 123 B and so on. This system lasted until 1983, the last registration in this format being ABC 123 Y. This was followed by putting the letter showing the year at the front of the number plate: A 123 ABC, B 123 ABC for 1984 and so on.

PRE 1963 PLATE

ABC **123**

Points: 25

FROM 1963

ABC **123** A

Points: 20

END OF 1983

ABC **123** Y

Points: 20

FROM 1983

A **123** ABC

Points: 15

This lasted until September 2001 when the first of the registration plates we see today appeared with two letters, then two numbers (showing the year) followed by three random letters. Cars are now registered twice a year – in March and September. Cars registered in March use the last two digits of the year (e.g. KX 16 ABC for March 2016), and cars registered in September use the last two digits of the year with 50 added (e.g. KX 66 ABC for September 2016). You will see some 'newer' cars with old, pre-1963 number plates (i.e. ABC 123). This is usually done to personalise the car, perhaps with the owner's initials, and these number plates are referred to as 'private number plates'. You will sometimes see these offered for sale, along with unusual modern number plates.

FROM 2001

AB51 ABC

Points: 10

2008 PLATE

AB58 ABC

Points: 10

2015/2016 PLATE

AB65 ABC

Points: 10

PERSONALISED

SHE11 A

Points: 10
score for any private or personalised plate

START OF MOTORWAY SIGN

Points: 5

After this point motorway rules apply.

 Points: 5

NO ENTRY SIGN

Stop! Do not go along this road, cars will be coming the other way.

SLIP ROAD

Points: 5

If you want to join the motorway you must first use a short piece of road known as a slip road. This allows you to get up to motorway speed before joining the main carriageway.

Points: 5

HARD SHOULDER

If a road is classed as a motorway it usually has a hard shoulder. Traffic is not permitted on this, except in case of breakdown or when instructed to do so.

NO HARD SHOULDER

Points: 10

No hard shoulder for 400 yards

Some motorways have limited space and do not have any room for a hard shoulder, typically around an obstruction such as a bridge.

Points: 5

MOTORWAY SPLITS

Major junctions where motorways split in two or more directions often have direction signs for two miles before to prepare drivers.

STEEL CENTRAL BARRIER

Points: 5

The central barrier in the middle of the motorway is a safety feature to help prevent cars travelling in opposite directions from hitting each other.

Points: 5

Cat's eyes were first used in 1933. Every time a car runs over one it 'cleans' the eye. They mark the centre of the road by reflecting headlights back to the driver at night.

DIRECTION SIGN

Points: 5

This sign gives drivers destination information about the next junction.

Points: 5

SERVICES

It is important to take regular breaks on a long road trip. Motorway service stations offer refreshments and toilet facilities. This sign tells you the next service area is 16 miles away with a second on a different motorway 22 miles away, and a third on that same motorway 27 miles away.

DISTANCE ON MOTORWAY

Points: 5

M1
The NORTH
Sheffield 32
Leeds 59

It is important to know how far it is to your destination and motorways provide regular updates on distances to the nearest major towns.

Points: 10

AIRPORT SIGN

Take this exit for the airport.

Points: 15

COUNTY BORDER

At this point you are passing into a new county.

COUNTRY BORDER

Points: 25

And at this one you are crossing into a new country!

DON'T DRIVE TIRED

Points: 15

Every year many accidents are caused by drivers who fall asleep at the wheel. This sign reminds the driver to take a break.

Points: 10

GRITTING

Gritting the roads helps to stop them from freezing in winter.

SOS PHONE

Points: 5

If drivers breakdown they can use these SOS phones to call for help. They are marked with a unique number so emergency services know where to send assistance.

SPEED CAMERA SIGN

Points: 5

This is a warning sign to alert drivers there are speed cameras ahead.

Points: 10

AVERAGE SPEED CAMERA

These cameras read the number plate of passing vehicles and measure their speed over a set distance.

SERVICES SIGN

Points: 10

This is one of the signs that informs drivers that the services are approaching.

Points: 5

FUEL STATION

You may need to refuel at the service station.

Points: 5

REFRESHMENTS

While you are at the services you many want to buy a drink or snack to take away, or you may have time to sit down and enjoy a meal in the restaurant.

PEOPLE SHOPPING

Most services have shops selling all kinds of things.

Points: 5

PICNIC AREA

If you have brought along your own picnic you could sit outside in the sunshine.

Points: 10

55

WORKS ACCESS SIGN

Points: 5

This is a works site entrance giving access to workers' vehicles only.

Points: 5

FREE RECOVERY

Roadworks are places where it is very easy for traffic to build up so to help move blockages as quickly as possible, if you break down while travelling through roadworks, a recovery truck will take you to safety for no charge.

DELAYS POSSIBLE UNTIL...

Points: 5

Night-time works 14 July to 26 July

Expect delays

Wherever there are roadworks there are often delays.

Points: 5

DIGGERS

Track diggers like this one are always used on major roadworks and road building schemes, so that huge chunks of material can be dug out in one go and the construction work can be carried out with the minimum of delay.

ROAD ROLLERS

Points: 10

Used to make the road surface smooth and flat.

NARROW LANES

While repairs are talking place there is often limited space so lane width is reduced.

 Points: 5

LANE CLOSED

Mobile lane closure signs warn drivers to keep to one side of the road.

 Points: 10

CONES

Points: 5

Roy Pedersen / Shutterstock.com

Cones are common sights on UK roads when roadworks are going on. They can be used to keep vehicles in lanes or to completely cut off some exits entirely. Some large sites use many thousands of cones over miles of roadworks.

Almost every car carries a logo, usually positioned on the front grille and the boot. Here are some that you might see.

ALFA ROMEO

Points: 15

ASTON MARTIN

Points: 30

AUDI

Points: 10

BMW

Points: 15

FERRARI

Frank11 / shutterstock.com

35 Points: 35 Top Spot!

FORD

JuliusKielaitis / Shutterstock.com

10 Points: 10

MERCEDES-BENZ

Alexander Tolstykh / Shutterstock.com

10 Points: 10

MITSUBISHI

Virbulus Kielaitis / shutterstock.com

15 Points: 15

NISSAN

Oliver Hoffmann / shutterstock.com

Points: 10

PEUGEOT

dean bertoncelj / shutterstock.com

Points: 10

PORSCHE

chomsltr / shutterstock.com

Points: 30

RENAULT

Arseniy Krasnevsky / shutterstock.com

Points: 10

SEAT

Points: 10

SMART

Points: 20

TOYOTA

Points: 10

VOLVO

Points: 10

INDEX

i-SPY

How to get your i-SPY certificate and badge

Let us know when you've become a super-spotter with 1000 points and we'll send you a special certificate and badge!

HERE'S WHAT TO DO!

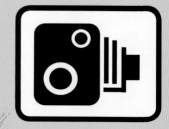

- ✓ Ask an adult to check your score.

- ✓ Visit www.collins.co.uk/i-SPY to apply for your certificate. If you are under the age of 13 you will need a parent or guardian to do this.

- ✓ We'll send your certificate via email and you'll receive a brilliant badge through the post!